THE GOLDEN RULES
OF
AMERICAN
FOOTBALL

THE GOLDEN RULES OF AMERICAN FOOTBALL

A CORGI BOOK 0 552 12600 4

First publication in Great Britain

PRINTING HISTORY
Corgi edition published 1985

Corgi Books are published by Transworld Publishers Ltd.,
Century House, 61-63 Uxbridge Road, Ealing, London W5 5SA,
in Australia by Transworld Publishers (Aust.) Pty. Ltd.,
26 Harley Crescent, Condell Park, NSW 2200, and in New
Zealand by Transworld Publishers (N.Z.) Ltd., Cnr. Moselle
and Waipareira Avenues, Henderson, Auckland.

Made and printed in Great Britain by
Hunt Barnard Printing Ltd., Aylesbury, Bucks.

The Player when reporting to training camp, usually in mid-July, should be in fairly good physical shape.

When a huddle breaks, each Player must go quickly to his assigned spot in the formation.

Offensive Linemen may benefit from wearing thick gloves, as their fingers and hands are prone to the battering of line play.

It is illegal for the Player to use adhesive on his uniform, equipment or any part of his body.

A kickoff is illegal unless it travels 10 yards or is touched by the receiving team.

The ball is an inflated rubber bladder in the shape of a prolate spheroid, filled with $12\frac{1}{2}$ to $13\frac{1}{2}$ pounds of air enclosed in a pebble-grained leather case.

For unnecessary roughness the penalty will be the loss of 15 yards.

On certain matters the Referee may consult with the Captain of the offending team.

In some weather conditions it may be more advantageous to throw the ball rather than kick it.

Kneeing an opponent will result in the loss of 15 yards (and disqualification if flagrant).

Filming and video play an important part in the game, and are useful in giving Players immediate feedback on their performances.

The penalty for a team's late arrival on the field prior to the scheduled kickoff will be 15 yards and loss of coin toss option.

It is essential for the serious Player to practise when and where possible.

The Head Coach will usually instruct the Quarter-back on what the next play should be, and to shout encouragement to the team.

Players must respect the decisions of Officials at all times.

In the huddle, the Quarterback calls the play. As it is so important, he should practice his calls to perfection.

No Player on offense may assist a Runner except by blocking for him.

A Player's number must be clearly visible and worn on the front, back and each shoulder of his shirt.

Illegal equipment will result in suspension from the game. The Player may return after one down when legally equipped.

The helmet is the most important part of the Player's equipment and he must ensure that it is of proven standard before wearing it in a game.

The Linebacker will watch the Ball-carrier at all times, ready to attack at the first opportunity.

Any intruder onto the field must be totally ignored by the Players.

It is important that the Wide Receiver gives himself as much space and height as possible when taking a catch.

In wet weather a Runner should try to keep the ball dry as it will be easier to pass or kick.

A greasy or wet ball can be difficult to throw.

All Players must wear a helmet, shoulder pads, hip pads, thigh pads, knee pads, stockings and acceptable shoes.

Only one ball may be in play at any one time.

It is illegal for a Ball Carrier to be clipped by an Opponent.

The Referee determines the legality of the snap and will position himself where he can observe the play without hindrance.

A Player may take instructions from the Coach to give to other Players.

The Referee shall decide on whether the conditions are suitable to play in.

Deliberate time-wasting will be penalized.

The head-slap is illegal and will be heavily penalized.

The Trainer must decide when an injury is serious enough to warrant an examination by a Doctor.

It is legal to pull at an Opponent's shirt, but no other article of clothing or gear must be pulled.

Clothing should be comfortable and not too tight.

For acts of unqualified violence and total disregard of authority, the Player is sent off for the rest of the game.

Some placekicks — field goals and extra points — require a Player to hold the ball for the Kicker.

The twisting, turning or pulling of an Opponent's face mask is dangerous and will be penalized by the loss of 15 yards.

Players should be in peak physical condition to go on to field.

The Player must endeavour to catch the ball cleanly and decisively.

Ungentlemanly conduct will be penalized by a loss of 15 yards with retention of down.

'Chucking' is the warding off of an opponent who is in front of a Defender. This is achieved by contacting him with a quick extension of the arm or arms.

45

A Kicker is not obliged to wear footwear.

A Trainer, like a Head Coach, is always on hand to listen or give advice to a Player.

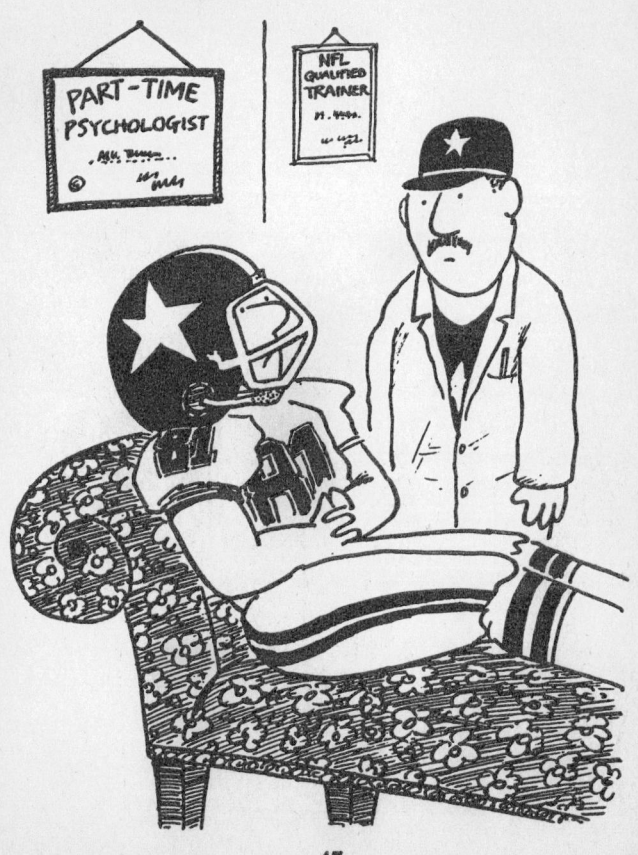

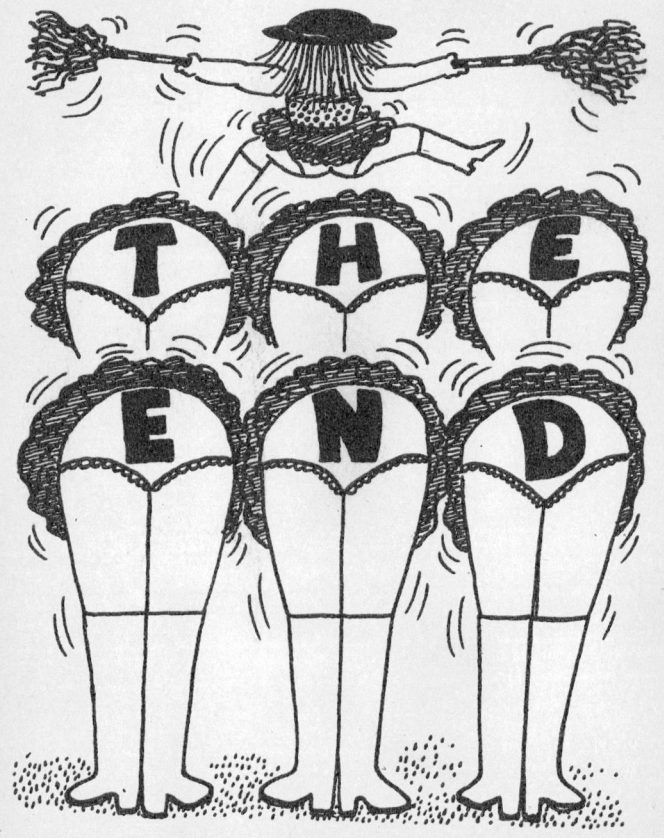